TELL ME HOW IT WORKS

HOW DO TELESCOPES WORK?

PHIL CORSO

PowerKiDS press
New York

Published in 2021 by The Rosen Publishing Group, Inc.
29 East 21st Street, New York, NY 10010

First Edition

Editor: Siyavush Saidian
Book Design: Reann Nye

Photo Credits: Cover Egor Valeev/Shutterstock.com; Series Art (gears) goodwin_x/Shutterstock.com; Series Art (newspaper) Here/Shutterstock.com; pp. 5, 11 AstroStar/Shutterstock.com; p. 6 Vadim Sadovski/Shutterstock.com; p. 7 Hulton Archive/Getty Images; p. 13 (HST) NASA/ Getty Images News/Getty Images; p. 13 (top) Photo 12/ Universal Images Group/Getty Images; p. 14 edobric/Shutterstock.com; p. 15 Joe McNally/ Hulton Archive/Getty Images; p. 17 Peter Dazeley/ DigitalVision/Getty Images; p. 19 Baltimore Sun/Tribune News Service/Getty Images; p. 21 (bottom) Bloomberg/Getty Images; p. 21 (top) ullstein bild Dtl./ ullstein bild/Getty Images.

Some of the images in this book illustrate individuals who are models. The depictions do not imply actual situations or events.

Library of Congress Cataloging-in-Publication Data

Names: Corso, Phil, author.
Title: How do telescopes work? / Phil Corso.
Description: New York : PowerKids Press, 2021. | Series: Tell me how it works | Includes bibliographical references and index.
Identifiers: LCCN 2019052491 | ISBN 9781725318212 (paperback) | ISBN 9781725318236 (library binding) | ISBN 9781725318229 (6 pack)
Subjects: LCSH: Telescopes–Juvenile literature.
Classification: LCC QB88 .C 2021 | DDC 522/.2–dc23
LC record available at https://lccn.loc.gov/2019052491

Manufactured in the United States of America

CPSIA Compliance Information: Batch #CSPK20. For Further Information contact Rosen Publishing, New York, New York at 1-800-237-9932.

CONTENTS

SCOPE IT OUT

Sometimes, things are so small, or so far away, they can't be seen with just the human eye. That's when a telescope comes in handy.

Telescopes are scientific tools made up of mirrors, or glass that reflects light, and **lenses** that make faraway things look bigger and brighter. When you look at something through a telescope, putting your eye to its lens, the object appears to be closer and clearer than it would be without the telescope.

Pressing your eye up to a telescope makes everything you can see look closer. To anyone on the other end, it makes your eyeball look bigger.

AN EYE ON HISTORY

It took a team of many people to get to today's modern telescopes. Dutch lens maker Hans Lippershey invented the first **refractor** telescope in 1608. It could show objects at three times their actual size.

TECH TALK

Telescopes are usually built for viewing what the human eye can naturally see, like other planets. There are other kinds that help us see **invisible** things, like radio waves.

The next year, Galileo Galilei heard about the Dutchman's invention and made a telescope of his own that could make objects look 20 times bigger. He used it to study space. In the late 1600s, Isaac Newton built the reflecting telescope, which uses mirrors instead of lenses to direct light.

BEHIND THE LENS

They all accomplish the same task, but there are several different kinds of telescopes.

Refracting telescopes use sets of different lenses to bend rays of light and make objects appear closer. Reflecting telescopes have mirrors inside that help you see faraway objects. One mirror takes the light from the object and reflects that light to another mirror, which sends the light to the eyepiece of the telescope, or the part that you look through. The eyepiece lens also acts as a **magnifier**.

Reflector telescopes use two mirrors in a short telescope tube to make images, or views, clearer.

REFLECTING TELESCOPE

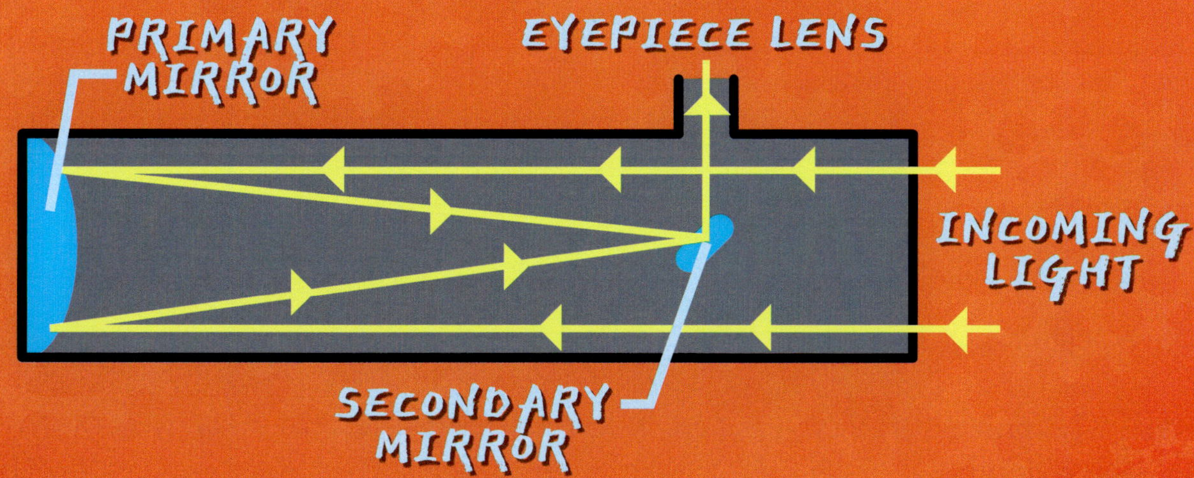

HOW THE TWO TYPES OF TELESCOPES WORK

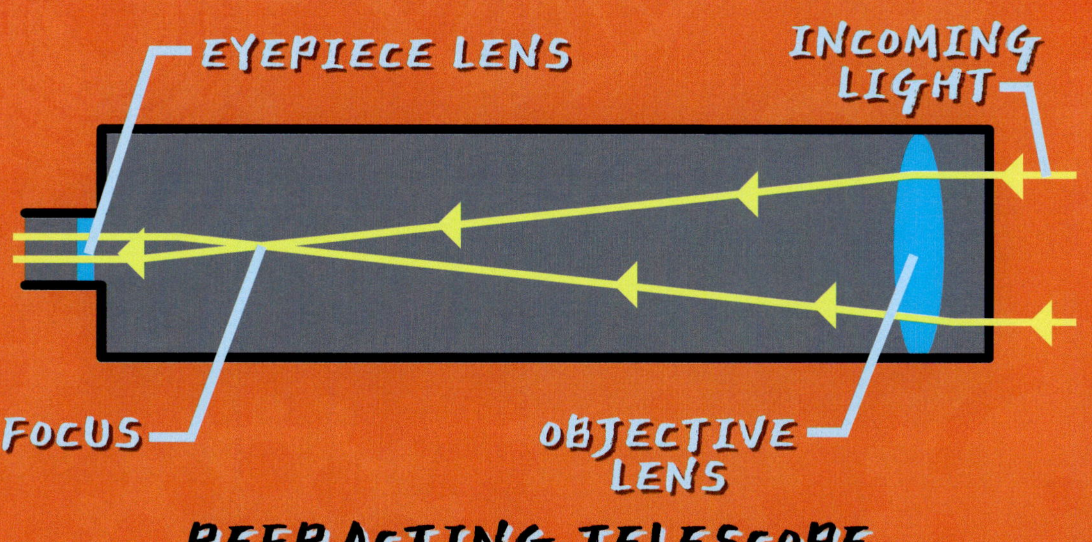

REFRACTING TELESCOPE

DIFFERENT SCOPES

Most telescopes are either the refractor or the reflector kind. While they both produce results that are close to the same, the two types have different features.

Refractor telescopes are long tubes with a lens in front and an eyepiece in the back. They're good for viewing certain planets and moons. Reflector telescopes are normally shorter and less expensive. They're good for viewing groups of objects, such as galaxies, or very large groups of stars. That's because they often have a wider aperture, or light-collecting area.

TECH TALK

In the 1960s, Raymond Davis Jr. made one of the weirdest telescopes ever. He used 600 tons (544 mt) of a cleaning liquid to find and watch tiny, invisible matter called neutrinos coming from the sun.

Not all telescopes are created equal, as they work in different ways and come in many different shapes and sizes.

SEEING CLEARLY

Telescopes have **evolved**. Scientists have found ways to combine the best features of refractors and reflectors. The catadioptric telescope, or compound telescope, was built in the 1930s. It uses both lenses and mirrors to create an image. Unlike refractor telescopes, they can be small.

Near the end of the 1900s, European and American space groups teamed up to build one of the biggest reflector telescopes of all: the Hubble Space Telescope (HST). It was launched, or sent, into Earth's **orbit** in 1990.

The HST drifts through space to this day, snapping images of space.

WITNESSING HISTORY

There have been many important telescope improvements over time. American scientist George Ellery Hale helped build the world's largest refracting telescope in the 1890s—its main lens is about 3 feet (1 m) wide! He also built the 60-inch (1.5 m) reflecting Mount Wilson telescope in 1908 and the 200-inch (5.1 m) Hale telescope.

TECH TALK

The **successor** to the HST is the James Webb Space Telescope, a large space-based reflecting telescope that can see **infrared** wavelengths. It's expected to be launched in 2021.

The VLA's 27 antennae take in radio signals, or messages, from throughout space.

New Mexico is home to the Very Large Array (VLA), built in 1980. This array, or group, has 27 radio antennae. The VLA and the HST have given scientists important **insights** into space.

MODERN DAY SCOPING

Though they were invented long ago, people still use telescopes today to see things they wouldn't normally see. Their uses range from basic to cutting-edge.

Binoculars are two hand-held, connected refractor telescopes that can be used to spot faraway objects and to find people who are in danger. More advanced telescopes help scientists discover new things about space. In 2019, the National Aeronautics and Space Administration (NASA) used the HST to find new galaxies.

Binoculars are telescopes too, and they can help save lives when used for things like finding ships that are in danger.

I SPY PROGRESS

Telescope technology has never stopped progressing, or improving. By the time you read this, telescopes will have already become more advanced than when this was written!

In 2019, NASA came up with ways to watch stars using telescopes and tiny shutters, or openings that let in light, that help them look at hundreds of galaxies at once. The group also tested a new sunshield system to shade the James Webb Space Telescope. This will help keep the telescope safe from the sun's heat and bright light.

TECH TALK

The word telescope is actually hundreds of years old. It comes from the Latin *tele*, which means faraway, and *skopos*, which means to examine or to look.

This model of the James Webb Space Telescope shows how far telescope advancements have come over many years.

A CLOSER LOOK INTO THE FUTURE

Scientists are always working on new telescopes. In the United States, NASA has several ongoing telescope programs.

At the beginning of 2020, NASA was working on a wide-angle infrared space telescope. Made from parts of an old telescope, it will be able to take pictures with a wide field of view, or area that can be seen by looking through it. Its field of view will be 100 times greater than HST's. It will also study the **atmospheres** of other planets. Another project called the LUVOIR would use a mirror six times wider than the HST's to study space.

TECH TALK

During the Apollo 11 moon landing in 1969, Pope Paul VI kept an eye on the moon by using a telescope before watching the moonwalk on TV.

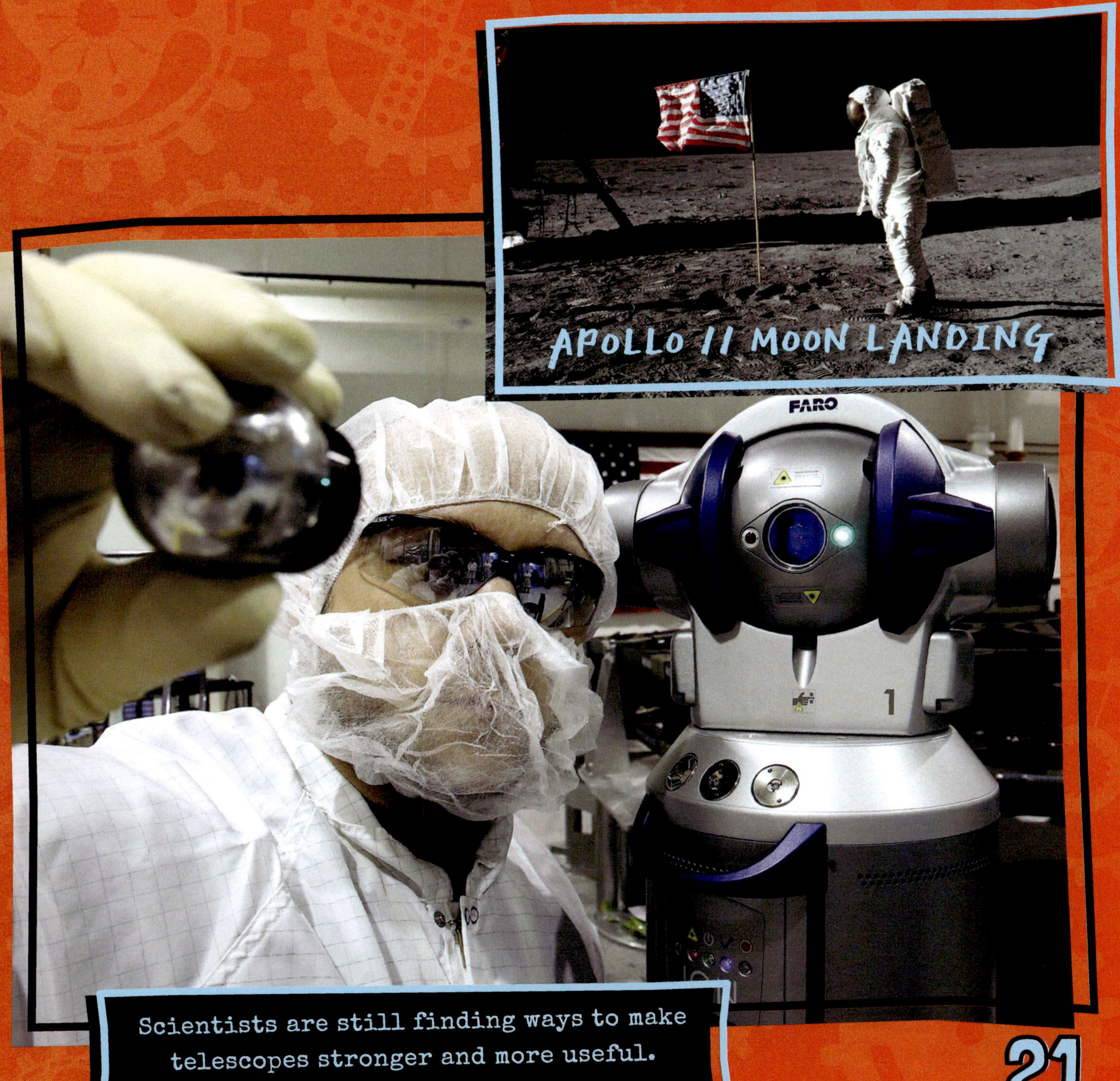

Scientists are still finding ways to make telescopes stronger and more useful.

MAKING IT WORK

There are many different branches of science. Physics involves the features of matter and energy, chemistry deals with what matter is made of, and biology is the study of living things. Telescopes bring these areas together. These tools use physics to reflect light, chemistry to study what makes up an atmosphere, and biology to search for life on other planets.

When it comes to learning more about the sky, for fun or for scientific discoveries, telescopes will continue to help people understand the stars and planets.

atmosphere: The envelope of gases surrounding the earth or another planet.

evolved: Grown and changed over time.

infrared: Referring to rays of light that people can't see and are longer than rays that produce red light.

insight: The capacity to gain an accurate and deep understanding of something.

invisible: Not able to be seen.

lens: A piece of glass or other transparent substance with curved sides for concentrating or dispersing light rays.

magnifier: Something that increases the size of an image.

orbit: The path taken by one body circling another.

refractor: A lens that causes refraction by changing the direction of light.

successor: A thing that succeeds another, or comes after.

Due to the changing nature of Internet links, PowerKids Press has developed an online list of websites related to the subject of this book. This site is updated regularly. Please use this link to access the list: www.powerkidslinks.com/tmhiw/telescopes